A TRUE BOOK

T0011266

GREEN ENERGY

Jasmine Ting

Children's Press®
An imprint of Scholastic Inc.

Content Consultant
Jeslin Varghese, LEED AP, WELL AP
President & Director of Sustainability
GBRI

Library of Congress Cataloging-in-Publication Data
Names: Ting, Jasmine (Journalist), author.
Title: Green energy / Jasmine Ting.
Description: First edition. | New York : Children's Press, an imprint of Scholastic Inc., 2024. | Series: A true book: a green future | Includes bibliographical references and index. | Audience: Ages 8–10. | Audience: Grades 4–6. | Summary: "This STEM-based set of True Books introduces students to the engineering innovations that can help us reach more environmentally friendly goals"— Provided by publisher.
Identifiers: LCCN 2023018945 (print) | LCCN 2023018946 (ebook) | ISBN 9781339020907 (library binding) | ISBN 9781339020914 (paperback) | ISBN 9781339020921 (ebk)
Subjects: LCSH: Renewable energy sources—Juvenile literature. | Clean energy industries—Juvenile literature. | Environmentalism—Juvenile literature. | BISAC: JUVENILE NONFICTION / Science & Nature / Environmental Conservation & Protection | JUVENILE NONFICTION / Science & Nature / General (see also headings under Animals or Technology)
Classification: LCC TJ808.2 .T56 2024 (print) | LCC TJ808.2 (ebook) | DDC 333.79/4—dc23/eng/20230426
LC record available at https://lccn.loc.gov/2023018945
LC ebook record available at https://lccn.loc.gov/2023018946

10 9 8 7 6 5 4 3 2 1   24 25 26 27 28
Printed in China 62
First edition, 2024

Design by Kathleen Petelinsek
Series produced by Spooky Cheetah Press

Front cover: People who work on wind turbines cannot be afraid of heights!

Find the Truth!

Everything you are about to read is true *except* for one of the sentences on this page.

Which one is **TRUE**?

T or F Humans have been able to harness the power of water for about 200 years.

T or F It is possible to extract energy from human waste.

Find the answers in this book.

What's in This Book?

The Hoover Dam
is the second-
tallest dam in
the United States.

Solar cells capture energy from the sun.

What Are We Waiting For?

Explore the challenges to switching to green energy.

A wind turbine can have as many as 8,000 parts!

INTRODUCTION

It takes **a lot of energy to power our lives**—and fossil fuels are the most common source of that energy. Fossil fuels are made from the remains of living things—like plants and animals—that died long ago. **Oil**, **coal**, and **natural gas** are all fossil fuels. They are nonrenewable forms of energy, which means that one day **they will run out**. Burning fossil fuels is also bad for our planet. When we burn oil, coal, or gas, heat-trapping **greenhouse gases** like carbon dioxide (CO_2) are released into the atmosphere. An increase in these gases in our atmosphere has caused a rise in Earth's surface temperature. That's called **global warming**, and it contributes to **climate change**.

Fossil fuels take millions of years to form. That's why there is a limited supply.

Factories that burn fossil fuels spew greenhouse gases into the air.

The good news is that things are changing. Thanks to advances in technology, we are slowly moving away from nonrenewable, polluting energy sources and increasing the use of **alternative energy** sources. Alternative, or "green," energy sources, like **the sun** and **the wind,** are **clean**. They release little to no greenhouse gases into the atmosphere. **Clean energy sources** are also **renewable**, which means they are natural. They do not run out like other kinds of energy sources. Read on to find out how green energy will play an **important role in the planet's future**.

Wind turbines and solar panels generate clean energy.

Green energy requires a lot of space. Big stretches of land are needed to build solar arrays, wind farms, and power plants. Wide-open spaces don't exist everywhere. And clearing land to make way for the development of these energies has other downsides, like destroying animals' natural habitat.

Green energy needs better storage. Solar and wind power are not constant. Energy from these sources needs to be stored in batteries. Then, when the sun isn't shining or the wind isn't blowing, users can draw power from the battery. The majority of the batteries used to store energy from these sources are still ineffective and lead to energy loss. Also, its manufacturing can have negative impacts on the environment.

Lake Mead formed behind the Hoover Dam. It is the largest human-made reservoir in the United States.

Construction of the Hoover Dam took place from 1930 to 1936.

Water at Work

Hydropower uses the flow of moving water to generate energy. It is one of the oldest sources of renewable energy we have. More than 2,000 years ago, people in Greece used waterwheels to grind wheat into flour. Today hydropower is most often used to generate electricity. In fact, it is the world's largest renewable source for electricity. The best-known hydroelectric power plant in the United States is the Hoover Dam on the Colorado River. This gigantic structure provides electricity for Southern California, Arizona, and Nevada. There are other ways to get energy from water too.

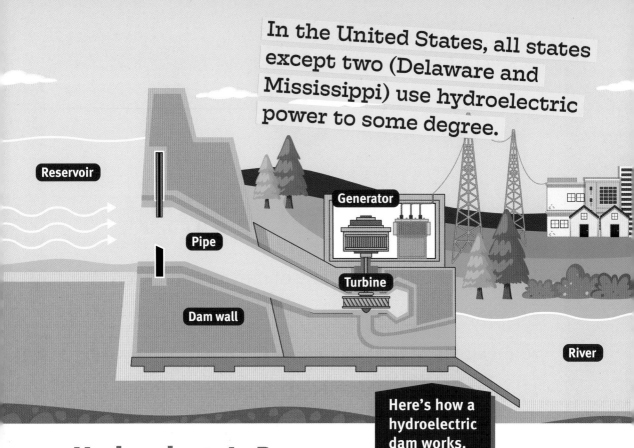

In the United States, all states except two (Delaware and Mississippi) use hydroelectric power to some degree.

Reservoir

Generator

Pipe

Turbine

Dam wall

River

Here's how a hydroelectric dam works.

Hydroelectric Power

Hydroelectric plants are usually located in dams by rivers. A dam is built across a river to block the flow of water. The water pools up behind gates in the dam, creating a reservoir. When those gates open, water rushes down through large pipes and causes turbines to spin, which generates electricity.

Flying Fish

Dams are great for generating electricity, but they can cause problems for wildlife. Many fish species swim up rivers in order to reproduce, and dams can block their way. That's why some dams have fish ladders. There are different designs, but all fish ladders function in a similar way. They are made up of a series of pools that work like stairs going up the side of the dam. Once the fish find the ladder entrance, they swim and jump from step to step. They keep doing this until they find their way out of the ladder and into the water beyond.

Salmon leap through the air to reach the next step of a fish ladder.

Using the Power of the Moon

Tides are the natural rise and fall of water levels in the ocean. They are caused by the moon's gravitational pull. The moving water creates energy that can be turned into electricity. It's called tidal power. Tidal power is not commonly used because it's more expensive to install than other green energy sources.

There are only about 10 operating tidal power plants worldwide.

If you have ever played in the ocean, you have felt the power of rushing water!

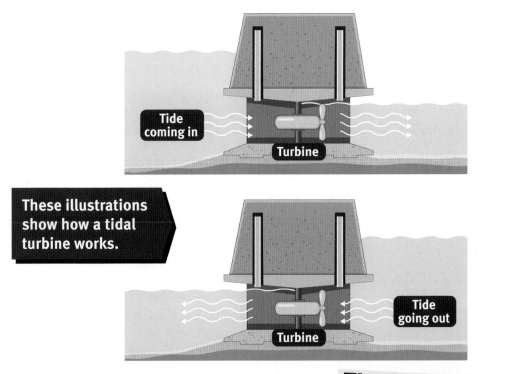

These illustrations show how a tidal turbine works.

Tide coming in

Turbine

Tide going out

Turbine

Tidal Power at Work

The largest tidal power plant is in South Korea.

A tidal turbine is one way to harness the power of moving water. The turbine is placed in a narrow channel between two bodies of water. When the tide comes in, the water rises on one side of the turbine and pours down through the other side, making the turbine move and generating electricity. When the tide goes out, the water on the higher side pours back to the lower side.

Splitting Water

Hydrogen is an **element** that can be used to create alternative energy. One way to produce it is with a process called water electrolysis. It uses electricity to split water **molecules** into hydrogen and oxygen. The hydrogen can then be captured and used as a fuel for a battery-like device called a fuel cell.

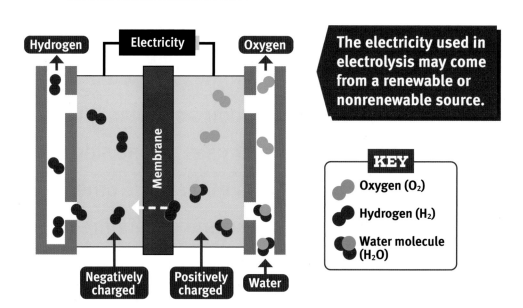

Water Electrolysis

Hydrogen | Electricity | Oxygen

Membrane

Negatively charged

Positively charged

Water

The electricity used in electrolysis may come from a renewable or nonrenewable source.

KEY

Oxygen (O₂)

Hydrogen (H₂)

Water molecule (H₂O)

The first 15,000 hydrogen-fueled cars on U.S. roads were all in California.

This BMW iX5 runs on hydrogen fuel.

Super Cells

Today there are cars that use hydrogen fuel cells instead of gas engines. Unlike traditional engines, fuel cells don't release greenhouse gases or pollutants. They release only water and small amounts of heat. Fuel cells are not commonly used, though. Hydrogen is more expensive to produce than other fuels. And the number of fueling stations for drivers to use is limited.

Green Technology Today

Green technology has come very far in recent years. A great example that shows this is the construction of more "green buildings," or buildings that are designed to be environmentally friendly and sustainable. They use less energy than other buildings, and they make their own energy using renewable sources. Every day, scientists and engineers are making more discoveries and innovations.

Timeline: Milestones in Green Energy Development

1842
William Grove, a Welsh scientist, invents the first hydrogen fuel cell.

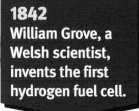

1882
The world's first hydroelectric power plant opens on the Fox River in Appleton, Wisconsin.

1883
American inventor Charles Fritts designs the first solar cell.

1887
Professor James Blyth makes the first windmill for electricity production. It powers his home in Scotland for 25 years.

Global Commitment

The U.S. National Climate Task Force has set ambitious goals for the United States in the coming years. One goal set for 2030 is to have reduced greenhouse gas **emissions** by more than 50 percent compared to 2005. Another is to reach 100 percent zero-carbon electricity generation by 2035. Other countries around the world have similar goals. With everyone working together, a green future is certainly within our reach.

1904
The first geothermal power plant is built in Tuscany, Italy.

1966
La Rance tidal power station in Brittany, France, opens. It is the longest-running tidal power station in the world.

TODAY
The U.S. currently has more than 2,500 solar power plants, more than 70,800 wind turbines, and close to 1,500 hydropower plants.

2030
Date by which renewable energy should provide 65 percent of the world's power.

The Land of Fire and Ice

Of all the countries in the world, Iceland is the closest to running completely on green energy. More than 99 percent of the nation's electricity comes from renewable sources. Part of Iceland's success is due to geography.

Water from the **Snaefellsjökull glacier** flows down the **Kirkjufellsfoss waterfall**. Hydroelectric power supplies 73 percent of the nation's electricity.

Waterfalls

Iceland has thousands of waterfalls and dozens of rivers that flow down from glaciers, which are a great source of hydroelectric power. Iceland is also home to hundreds of volcanoes and many natural hot springs, which make it rich in geothermal power. Let's take a look at some of the natural resources that make Iceland a leader in sustainable energy use.

Hot springs

Volcanoes

Volcanoes like **Mount Fagradalsfjall** (pictured), which erupted in 2022, show how much heat lies beneath the surface in Iceland. Almost 27 percent of electricity in Iceland is created from geothermal energy.

The **Blue Lagoon** is one of Iceland's most famous attractions. It is a spa located near the city of Reykjavik with pools, saunas, and steam rooms. It runs completely on geothermal energy. Nine out of 10 houses in Iceland are directly heated with geothermal water.

Ways to Live Green

We don't always have a say in how our energy is produced. And sometimes we have no choice but to rely on fossil fuels. But you can still reduce the impact your energy use has on the environment. Here are some easy ways to do that.

Lights Off!

During the day, when it's bright outside, use the sun's natural light rather than turning on electric lights. If you are using electric lights, remember to turn them off when you leave a room.

Shorten Showers

Limiting your time in the shower saves water. It also lessens the amount of energy needed to heat the shower water.

Unplug

Appliances, devices, and chargers that are not in use are still pulling energy from outlets. Don't leave these energy vampires plugged in.

Take a Ride

If your school is only a few blocks away, or you're meeting friends in your neighborhood, consider walking or riding a bike instead of asking for a ride in a car.

Shut Down Screens

Spending less time in front of screens and less time using devices means less electricity used.

Dress for Success

If you're feeling chilly at home, throw on a hoodie or some sweats rather than asking an adult to turn up the heat. The same goes for when it's hot inside—change into shorts and a tee before asking for air-conditioning. Open the windows and let fresh air in.

Carbon dioxide emissions from fossil fuels worldwide in 2021: 37.12 metric tons (37,120 kilograms)

Goal date for the world to have switched to 100 percent green energy: 2050

Global cost to go green by 2050: $4 trillion

Amount of energy from the sun that constantly hits Earth: 173,000 terawatts (trillions of watts)

Height of the tallest wind turbine in the world (Vestas in Denmark): 919 feet (280 meters)

Global electricity made from hydroelectric power in 2021: 15 percent

Global electricity made from wind power in 2021: 6.6 percent

Global electricity made from solar power in 2021: 3.6 percent

Did you find the truth?

(F) Humans have been able to harness the power of water for about 200 years.

(T) It is possible to extract energy from human waste.

Resources

Other books in this series:

You can also look at:

Brearley, Laurie. *Alternative Energy: Geothermal Power*. New York: Scholastic, 2019.

Brearley, Laurie. *Alternative Energy: Solar Power*. New York: Scholastic, 2019.

Brearley, Laurie. *Alternative Energy: Water Power*. New York: Scholastic, 2019.

Igini, Martina. *"What Is Renewable Energy?"* Earth.Org for Kids, March 31, 2022.

Ziem, Matthew. *Alternative Energy: Wind Power*. Scholastic, 2019.

Glossary

carbon neutral (KAHR-buhn NOO-truhl) having or resulting in no net addition of carbon dioxide to the atmosphere

climate change (KLYE-mit CHAYNJ) global warming and other changes in the weather and weather patterns that are happening because of human activity

element (EL-uh-muhnt) a substance that cannot be divided up into simpler substances

emissions (i-MISH-uhnz) substances released into the atmosphere

generator (JEN-uh-ray-tur) a machine that produces electricity by turning a magnet inside a coil of wire

molecules (MAH-luh-kyoolz) the smallest units that a chemical compound can be divided into that still display all of its chemical properties

renewable (ri-NOO-uh-buhl) able to be replaced by natural cycles

sustainable (suh-STAY-nuh-buhl) done in a way that can be continued and that doesn't use up natural resources

turbines (TUR-buhnz) engines powered by water, steam, wind, or gas passing through the blades of wheels and making them spin

Index

Page numbers in **bold** indicate illustrations.

About the Author

Jasmine Ting is a Filipino journalist based in New York City. Her work has been published in magazines, including *Scholastic News*. She enjoys telling stories about important events, recent trends, and people doing amazing things around the globe. She hopes her writing inspires young readers to learn more about the world around them. *Green Energy* is Jasmine's first book.